DISCOVER Yorkshire

John Potter

CONTENTS

MYRIAD

West Yorkshire

West Yorkshire stretches from the Pennines in the west to the lowlands on the edge of the Vale of York. The region contains a clutch of wonderful towns and cities, from the great conurbations of Leeds and Bradford to the regional centres of Halifax, Huddersfield and Wakefield and the market towns of Keighley, Pontefract and Wetherby. But all of the region is not urban – West Yorkshire is dotted with villages and great houses such as Harewood House and Temple Newsam.

◀▼ **Leeds** The commercial capital of Yorkshire is dominated by the Town Hall, built between 1853-58. It is topped by a magnificent domed clocktower rising to 225ft (68m). The gilded owl (shown below, with the clock tower behind) stands beside the Civic Hall, built between 1931-33. The market hall (left) was built in 1904 at the junction of Kirkgate and Vicar Lane. Leeds Waterfront (below) was the dockland area at the termini of the two canals – the Aire and Calder Navigation and the Leeds and Liverpool. By the 1960s, this area was run-down. Many of the old warehouses have now been converted and new apartment blocks constructed.

◀ **Harewood House** This magnificent house, the home of Earl and Countess Lascelles, was built by the York architect John Carr between 1759 and 1772 on the instructions of Edwin Lascelles whose father had made his fortune in the ribbon trade, from his position as collector of customs in Barbados and his directorship of the East India Company. The interiors were the work of Robert Adam and much of the furniture is by Thomas Chippendale. In the 1840s the south façade was remodelled by Sir Charles Barry, the architect of the Houses of Parliament. The grounds were laid out by Lancelot "Capability" Brown who dammed Gawthorpe Beck to create a serpentine lake. To the south is an ornamental garden. Still the home of the Lascelles family, Harewood is one of Yorkshire's major attractions.

◄▲ **Bradford**'s magnificent neo-Gothic Town Hall (left) dates from 1873 and reflects the city's prominence and ambition as a commercial centre, worthy of being ranked with other cities such as Liverpool and Glasgow. Re-named City Hall in 1965, its frontage overlooks Centenary Square which is graced with sculptures of British monarchs, including Oliver Cromwell – an echo of Bradford's role in the Civil War. The Alhambra Theatre (above) was built in 1914 for the musical impresario Frank Laidler, the "King of Pantomime". It was restored in 1986 after suggestions that it might be demolished and a car park built in its place.Two of Bradford's surviving medieval buildings are the Cathedral and Bolling Hall. Now a museum, and just a mile from the city centre, Bolling Hall gives visitors an insight into the lives and times of the two families for whom it provided a home over five hundred years. During the Civil War the household supported the Royalist cause.

Halifax Seven miles south-west of Bradford, Halifax is the capital of Calderdale. The town owes its prosperity to the wool trade and its town hall was designed by Sir Charles Barry. The Piece Hall (detail below) completed in 1779, contains more than 300 rooms built around an open quadrangle; it was here that handloom weavers living in outlying cottages brought their "pieces" of woollen cloth to sell. The Wainhouse Tower was built for John Edward Wainhouse to carry the smoke and fumes produced by his dye works out of the Calder valley. At 253ft (77m) high it is one of Calderdale's best-loved landarks. Other Halifax attractions include the Victoria Theatre which dates from 1901; originally a concert hall it was converted into a theatre in 1960. The Eureka! hands-on children's museum is located in the railway station. It has interactive displays on the natural world, the human body and commerce and industry.

Huddersfield The West Riding town of Huddersfield boasts 1,660 listed buildings – only Westminster and Bristol have more. One of the town's most famous sons was the Labour prime minister Harold Wilson. His statue was erected in 1999 and graces St George's Square in front of the railway station. Built between 1847-48, the station has been called "a stately home with trains in it". Its Classical facade is 416ft long and is supported by eight 68ft high columns. The roof of the town's magnificent open-air market is supported by cast-iron pillars (detail left). The magnificent town hall doubles as a concert hall and is home to Huddersfield's renowned choral society.

Haworth The Brontë Parsonage Museum (left) is Haworth's major attraction. When the Rev Patrick Brontë brought his family to live at the parsonage in 1820 the village was little more than a cluster of stone cottages clinging to a steep hill, with the church at the top of the street and the moors stretching into the distance. The Parsonage is full of paintings, books and papers that belonged to the Brontës and the rooms have been restored to convey what life was like for the parson and his family. The village (above) retains its Victorian air with cobbled streets, an old-fashioned apothecary's shop, booksellers and antique shops. Visitors can make their way to the Brontë Falls and Top Withens on the moors. The setting of this farmhouse, now in ruins, is thought to have inspired Emily Brontë's *Wuthering Heights*.

Castle Hill The hill fort at Almondbury near Huddersfield, seen here from Farnley Tyas, is made up of a series of Iron Age and medieval earthworks. The flat-topped hill has been the site of Chartist rallies as well as prize-fighting. The Victoria or Jubilee tower was added in 1899 to celebrate Queen Victoria's Diamond Jubilee. The remains of an anti-aircraft battery can still be seen near the south-west corner of the hill.

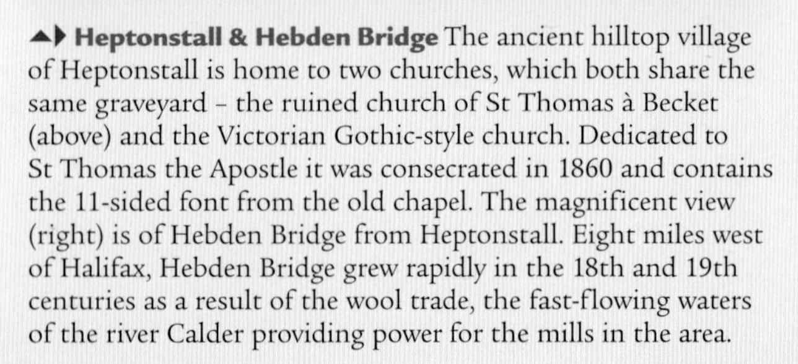

Heptonstall & Hebden Bridge The ancient hilltop village of Heptonstall is home to two churches, which both share the same graveyard – the ruined church of St Thomas à Becket (above) and the Victorian Gothic-style church. Dedicated to St Thomas the Apostle it was consecrated in 1860 and contains the 11-sided font from the old chapel. The magnificent view (right) is of Hebden Bridge from Heptonstall. Eight miles west of Halifax, Hebden Bridge grew rapidly in the 18th and 19th centuries as a result of the wool trade, the fast-flowing waters of the river Calder providing power for the mills in the area.

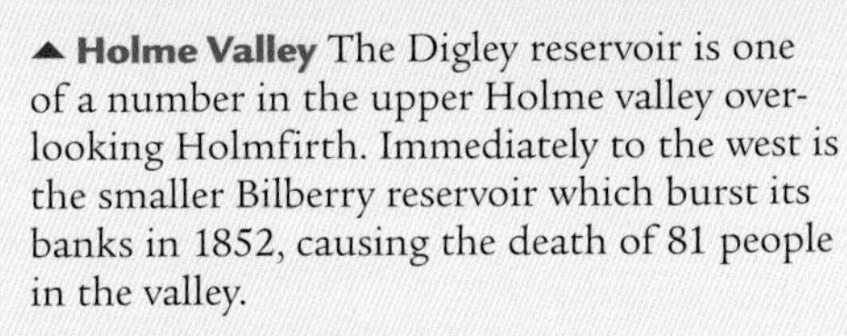

▲ **Holme Valley** The Digley reservoir is one of a number in the upper Holme valley overlooking Holmfirth. Immediately to the west is the smaller Bilberry reservoir which burst its banks in 1852, causing the death of 81 people in the valley.

▼▶ **Holmfirth** This picturesque Pennine town developed rapidly in the 16th century thanks to the burgeoning cloth industry and its local slate and stone mines. Now the town and its surrounding countryside are best-known as the setting for the long-running television series *Last of the Summer Wine*. Thousands of tourists flock to the area each year to enjoy the scenery and hoping to identify locations used in the series. Sid's Café (right) in the town centre, a watering hole familiar to all fans, is now a place of pilgrimage. Next door to the character Nora Batty's fictional house in the series is the Summer Wine exhibition (bottom) which combines the Wrinkled Stocking Tea Room and a re-creation of the character Compo's home.

The Dales

Straddling the Pennines, the Yorkshire Dales National Park is an area of outstanding natural beauty where pretty villages nestle amidst the typical Dales scenery of drystone walls and barns or close to stark limestone escarpments. The grandeur of the Three Peaks, the scenic Settle to Carlisle railway line and the outstanding limestone scenery of Malhamdale are all to be found in this region. The beautiful Wensleydale village of West Burton (below) is famous for its falls, which are a popular location for artists and photographers.

▸ **East Gill Force** This magnificent waterfall is situated just 10 minutes stroll from the small village of Keld which nestles snugly at the head of Swaledale. The waterfall is to the north of the Pennine Way where the long-distance footpath crosses East Stonesdale. Keld's pretty cottages are clustered around a tiny square. The village name derives from the old Norse word *keld*, meaning "spring" and the nearby Swale is fed by many small becks which flow down from the surrounding fells.

▴ **Richmond** The capital of Swaledale, Richmond is dominated by its castle keep, part of the massive castle built by Alan the Red of Brittany, a trusted supporter of William I. Richmond ranks among the most beautiful towns in England, with many elegant Georgian houses, cobbled streets and pretty cottage gardens. At the centre of the impressive marketplace is the 12th century chapel of the Holy Trinity, now used as the regimental museum of the Green Howards. In 1788, Samuel Butler, a local actor and manager, built the Theatre Royal, a beautiful Georgian theatre, which is still in use today.

◂ **Gunnerside** The beautiful windswept fells and attractive patchwork of fields, drystone walls and barns along the valley bottom make this part of Swaledale a favourite with visitors. In early summer the wildflower meadows are a vibrant sea of colour, and a delight to walk through. Gunnerside Gill runs through the tiny village of Gunnnerside and meets the river just below The King's Head inn.

▾ **Kisdon Hill** Swaledale is one of the more remote northern dales, to the west of Richmond. The limestone mass of Kisdon Hill stands at the head of Swaledale. This viewpoint looks south towards Muker.

▲ **Askrigg** Just one mile north-east of Bainbridge on the northern side of Wensleydale, Askrigg is a tiny settlement best known as the setting for the popular television series *All Creatures Great and Small.* In the town centre, the King's Arms appeared in the series as the Drover's Arms. Above the village sits Askrigg Common and beyond it the unmistakable form of Addlebrough. Askrigg was a former medieval market town and is now popular with walkers and daytrippers.

▲ **Aysgarth Falls** Situated seven miles west of Leyburn, Aysgarth is best known for the spectacular waterfalls on the Ure that cascade down a series of limestone steps. Riverside walks link the Upper, Middle and Lower Falls which are all within a mile of each other. The best view of the Upper Force is from the 16th century bridge in the centre of the village.

◀ **Castle Bolton** Dominated by Bolton Castle, the small village of Castle Bolton is five miles west of Leyburn. This massive fortress has loomed over Wensleydale since 1379 and is one of the country's best preserved castles; Mary Queen of Scots was imprisoned here in 1568 and 1569. In the middle of the village is a wide green and St Oswald's, the attractive 14th century church, nestles in the shadow of the castle.

▼ **Dent** Although it lies within the Yorkshire Dales National Park the pretty village of Dent is actually in Cumbria, four miles south-east of Sedbergh. The white-painted cottages are very Cumbrian in character in contrast to the warm stone buildings usually found in the lower Yorkshire Dales.

◀ **Middleham** Situated just two miles from Leyburn between Coverdale and Wensleydale, Middleham is dominated by its castle, built around 1170 by Robert Fitz Randolph during the reign of Henry II. The massive central keep has 12ft (3.5m) thick walls and is one of the largest in England.

▼ **Ribblehead Viaduct** The 72-mile Settle-Carlisle railway line is one of the most picturesque in Britain and runs through Ribblesdale offering dramatic views of Whernside and Pen-y-Ghent. Built in the 1870s, the line was renovated and re-opened in 2000. The magnificent 24-arch Ribblehead Viaduct to the north-west of Ribblehead station is seen here from Runscar Hill.

◀▲▶ Malham The extraordinary limestone landscape of Malhamdale is a great attraction for visitors and walkers. It was formed over millions of years, first as a result of glacial erosion and then by the effects of wind, rain and frost. Three of the best examples – the limestone cliff at Malham Cove, Malham Tarn and Gordale Scar – are sited behind the attractive village of Malham (left). Above the Cove lies Malham pavement (right), where hundreds of limestone blocks or "clints" are indented by deep fissures or "grykes".

▲ **Great Whernside** Wharfedale and Nidderdale run parallel to each other in a north-west to south-easterly direction. The rugged fell of Great Whernside dominates the skyline east of Buckden. Not to be confused with Whernside (one of the Three Peaks further west) it reaches a height of 2,310ft (705m) and creates an abrupt change from the lush pastures below. The long boulder-strewn ridge gives extensive views across Nidderdale to the east and westward to Wharfedale.

◀ **Halton Gill** Sheltered by Plover Hill, Cow Close Fell and Horse Head Moor, Halton Gill sits beside the infant river Skirfare with its attractive packhorse bridge. ▶ **Scalebar Force** is a cascading waterfall in a deeply wooded valley just outside Settle, on the road to Kirkby Malham. During wet weather the pretty rivulet changes into a raging torrent. The word "force", a Yorkshire dialect word for a waterfall, comes from the old Norse word *fors*, which is sometimes corrupted to "foss".

▲ **Buckden** The annual Buckden Pike Fell Race starts and finishes on the gala field in Buckden. The event draws runners from across the north of England, and watching them aiming for the top of Buckden Pike (2,303ft/702m) is a great spectacle. At the summit is a poignant memorial to the Polish crew of an aircraft that crashed here in 1942. Just one man survived – he made it to safety by following the tracks of a fox in the snow.

▲ **Wharfedale** Running from north to south, from the high moors of Langstrothdale to Ilkley, Wharfedale is one of the Dales' longest and most beautiful valleys. The stunning landscape of Wharfedale is revealed in this view from Rowan Tree Crag looking towards Hartlington Hall and Kail Hill, just east of Burnsall.

▼ **Burnsall** Ten miles north-west of Ilkley, the picturesque village of Burnsall is famous for the massive five-arched bridge (built on the site of a former packhorse bridge) which spans the meandering river Wharfe. Every August, the village hosts a feast and sports day - the Burnsall Feast Sports - which includes England's oldest fell race.

▸ Appletreewick This peaceful Wharfedale village four miles south-east of Grassington rests on a steep slope overlooked by the craggy summit of Simon's Seat. The main street is lined by ornate and characterful cottages with High Hall at the top and Low Hall at the bottom. The original owner of High Hall was Appletreewick's most famous inhabitant, Sir William Craven. Known as "Dick Whittington of the Dales" he was the son of a local farmer who was sent to London to make his fortune and eventually became Lord Mayor of the City in 1610. Loyal to his roots, Willam returned to Appletreewick and rebuilt High Hall.

◂ Bolton Priory This beautiful Augustinian priory is a stone's throw from the village of Bolton Bridge five miles west of Skipton. The magnificent ruins are immensely popular with visitors who enjoy picnicking and strolling along the banks of the river Wharfe. Close by, the river gushes in a thunderous cascade though a narrow chasm known as "the Strid". Further upstream, along a nature trail, is Barden Bridge and the beautifully sited Barden Tower, which was built in 1485 by Lord Henry Clifford.

▾ Jervaulx Abbey Situated between Masham and Leyburn are the ruins of this atmospheric Cistercian abbey. Dating from 1156 the abbey fell into ruin after the Dissolution in 1537. Enough remains of the ivy-covered crumbling walls to remind us of the simple yet austere lives of the "white monks". A weathered effigy of the abbey's great benefactor, Hugh Fitzhugh, stands in the grounds. It is thought that the monks at Jervaulx first perfected the recipe for Wensleydale cheese.

Vale of York

This large region stretches from the river Tees in the north to Selby in the south and from the eastern edge of the Yorkshire Dales in the west to the Yorkshire Wolds in the east. The Vale of York is largely made up of low-lying, undulating countryside. It is a rich agricultural area with hay meadows along the river floodplains and large fields intensively cultivated for arable crops. The region includes the busy market towns of Northallerton, Knaresborough and Thirsk, the elegant spa town of Harrogate and the cathedral cities of York and Ripon. Not only is it famous for farming but it is well-loved by the horse-racing fraternity with famous racecourses at York, Doncaster and Thirsk.

York Sited at the confluence of the rivers Ouse and Foss, this ancient city has had a turbulent history. Founded by the Romans, it suffered Viking invasion, was ravaged by William the Conqueror and became a major Royalist stronghold during the English Civil War. The city's eventful past is reflected in the many important historic buildings packed within its city walls: attractions such as York Minster (right), the narrow medieval streets around its core which include the famous Shambles, together with the Jorvik Viking Centre and the York Castle Museum have made the city one of the most popular tourist destinations in the UK. York has the longest and best-preserved town walls in Europe and there are 45 towers and four gateways (or "bars") at intervals along its length. A walk along the top of the wall is an ideal way to view the city.

▶ **York Minster** The largest Gothic cathedral in northern Europe, York Minster is the seat of the Archbishop of York, the second highest office in the Church of England. There has been a church here since 627; work on the current Minster began in 1220 and was not completed until 1472. York Minster is famous for the Great East window, completed in 1408, the largest expanse of medieval stained glass in the world.

◀ **Lendal Bridge** This elegant iron bridge, with stone towers at either end, was built by Thomas Page in 1863. It is one of nine bridges over the river Ouse in York.

▲ **The Shambles** One of York's highlights is the Shambles, a meandering medieval street leading up to the Minster. Today it is filled with souvenir shops; in the Middle Ages it was home to many butchers (the name comes from the Anglo-Saxon words *shammels* or *flesh-shammels* meaning an open-air slaughterhouse). Most of the buildings along the Shambles are medieval but there are also some outstanding Tudor half-timbered houses.

▼ **Clifford's Tower** This stone fortification in Tower Street is all that remains of the 13th and 14th century keep of York Castle. In 1190 it was the site of the massacre of 150 of the city's Jewish population who took refuge from attack by a mob in the wooden tower.

▲ **Knaresborough** This beautiful town grew up around the steep sides of the gorge of the river Nidd. It has been a strategic point for centuries and during the Middle Ages Knaresborough was firmly established on the royal circuit. The Norman castle was used as a hideout by the four knights who murdered Thomas à Becket in 1170. It was badly damaged during the Civil War when the Parliamentarians besieged the Royalists here and ordered its destruction. The castle's remains are open to the public and its grounds are used as a performance space – in particular for events during the Knaresborough Festival every August.

◀▶ **Harrogate** The first mineral spring was discovered at the Tewitt Well in this North Yorkshire town in 1571. By the 18th century, Harrogate had become a fashionable spa to rival Bath and Buxton. The Royal Pump Room has been converted into a museum telling its story. Close by are Valley Gardens (right) where many of the original wells were found. Bettys and Taylors opened the first of its "continental-style Tea Rooms" on Cambridge Circus (left) in 1919.

▲ **Castle Howard** Set amongst magnificent parkland 25 miles north-east of York, Castle Howard was built to a design by John Vanburgh from 1699-1712. This opulent residence is, along with Blenheim near Oxford, regarded as a masterpiece of English Baroque architecture. It gained fame with television audiences when it was used as the setting for *Brideshead Revisited*, the 1981 adaptation of Evelyn Waugh's celebrated novel.

▶ **Newby Hall** Sir Christopher Wren guided the design of Newby Hall, near Ripon, built in 1697. Since 1748 it has been home to the Compton family, whose ancestor William Weddell bought the property and enlarged it during the 1760s. The interior was remodelled by a variety of architects, including Robert Adam. The present grounds were laid out in the 1920s, with herbaceous borders and a dramatic broad grass walk leading down to the river Ure.

North York Moors

With its heather-clad moorland, fertile dales and characterful villages and market towns, this region has one of Yorkshire's most beautiful and captivating landscapes. One of the finest upland landscapes in Britain, the North York Moors include the north-east corner of Yorkshire stretching northwards from the Vale of Pickering to the border with County Durham and from the Hambleton and Cleveland Hills in the west to the coast.

▼Blakey Ridge The famous Lyke Wake Walk, a long-distance footpath, traverses the east to west watershed of the North York Moors through remote and mostly uninhabited moorland, passing Bronze Age burial mounds and lonely prehistoric standing stones en route.

▲ Roseberry Topping Dominating the countryside around Guisborough is the distinctive half-coned shape of Roseberry Topping. The hill's shape is due to the fact that half the summit has collapsed, owing to a geological fault or because many old alum or ironstone mines lie close to the top. On nearby Easby Moor there is a monument to Captain Cook who went to school in nearby Great Ayton.

▶ Mallyan Spout The highest waterfall on the North York Moors, Mallyan Spout, near Goathland, cascades 60ft (18m) down the side of West Beck Gorge. A short walk along the beck just to the right of the Mallyan Spout Hotel leads to the waterfall. In wet weather, spray is blown across the path giving visitors the impression of walking through a waterfall.

▲ **Hutton-le-Hole** Home to the Ryedale Folk Museum, this beautiful village is a popular stopping-off point for visitors. Its broad village green, dotted with moorland sheep, is an ideal spot for a summer picnic. The Folk Museum, Yorkshire's leading open-air museum, depicts north Yorkshire's past.

▶ **Rosedale** This is a long, extended valley which stretches out in a south-easterly direction from Westerdale Moor and Danby High Moor towards Hartoft End and Cropton Forest. The river Seven flows throughout its length and there are superb views across the dale from the road near the Lion Inn on Blakey Ridge. The Rosedale Show is held every August in the delightful village of Rosedale Abbey.

▲ **Sutton Bank** The Hambleton Escarpment rises abruptly to a height of around 1,000ft (305m), giving views of more than 30 miles. Roulston Scar and Hood Hill lie to the left. A short walk along the escarpment leads to Whitestone Cliff on the 110-mile Cleveland Way.

▲ **Rievaulx Abbey** The ruins of this Cistercian abbey in the narrow Rye valley show that this was once one of the finest monastic churches in northern Britain. Fine views of the abbey can be enjoyed from the Rievaulx Terrace and Temples which are situated on an escarpment high above the valley.

▶ **Hole of Horcum** Hollowed out of the heather-clad moor beside the Pickering to Whitby road, the Hole of Horcum is a huge natural amphitheatre. Legend has it that "the devil's punchbowl" was created by a giant named Wade who scooped out the rocks and earth, tossing them two miles east to Blakey Topping. A popular circular walk from the roadside car park passes this derelict farm cottage at Low Horcum.

The Coast

The eastern boundary of the North York Moors National Park is known as the North Yorkshire Heritage Coast. This is a beautiful and varied area with high rugged cliffs, traditional fishing villages, small river inlets and wide sandy bays. The Heritage Coast includes the resorts of Sandsend, Runswick Bay, Whitby, Robin Hood's Bay and Ravenscar. Further south are the long-established holiday resorts of Scarborough, Bridlington, Filey, Hornsea and Withernsea, interspersed with some of the finest cliff scenery on the east coast of Britain at Flamborough Head and Bempton Cliffs.

◀ **Ravenscar** One of the wildest and most exposed places on the Yorkshire coast, the steeply rising ground at Ravenscar climbs to form a grassy plateau almost 600ft (182m) above sea level. Ravenscar is sometimes referred to as "the town that never was". In 1895, the Ravenscar Estate Company planned to build a new town here to challenge the resorts of Whitby and Scarborough but the idea was abandoned due to the bitingly cold winds. There are fabulous views of Robin Hood's Bay from around the area, particularly from the coastal clifftop path, part of the Cleveland Way.

▶ **Robin Hood's Bay** South of Whitby, this picturesque fishing village has a series of winding streets and narrow alleyways (ginnels) lined with old houses and cottages, many with distinctive red pantiled roofs. In the 18th century, the bay was a centre for smuggling and there are a number of secret tunnels below the houses so that the smugglers could bring their illegal contraband ashore safely. From the surrounding countryside towards Ravenscar there are panoramic views across the bay.

▲ **Whitby** At the centre of what is often referred to as "Captain Cook Country", Whitby has the only natural harbour between the Tees and the Humber and is where the young James Cook learned the seafarer's trade. The house in Grape Lane where he served his apprenticeship is now a museum. The town's skyline is dominated by the ruins of St Hilda's Abbey, high on the east cliff next to the parish church of St Mary. The 199 steps that connect the parish church of St Mary to the town are a local institution. These "church stairs" were used to carry coffins up to the church; along the way there are resting places for the pall-bearers.

Bridlington With two glorious long sandy beaches, miles of elegant promenades and a very pretty and bustling harbour Bridlington has all the ingredients for the perfect holiday resort. Flamborough Head and its lighthouse are clearly visible from the north pier and beach. The town is divided into two parts, the old town about a mile inland and the holiday resort and fishing port at the quay fringing Bridlington Bay. The town's first hotel opened in 1805 and Bridlington soon became a firm favourite with the city-dwellers of West Yorkshire. The "Beside the Seaside Exhibition" close to the harbour contains fascinating exhibits of the town in its heyday.

Runswick Bay Colourful fishing boats called cobles are moored on the sandy beach at Runswick Bay, one of the Heritage Coast's most beautiful villages, much-loved by artists and holidaymakers. Access to the beach is by a steep 1-in-4 road.

Scarborough This elegant town is one of the north of England's most popular coastal towns and was Britain's first seaside resort. The ruined Norman castle and its headland stand 150ft (46m) above the harbour and dominate Scarborough's skyline, dividing the town into North Bay and South Bay. One of the best views of the town and headland is from Oliver's Mount just above the town's spa complex with its superb parks, theatres and conference hall. Anne Brontë died in Scarborough at the age of 28 and is buried in St Mary's church.

▲ **Flamborough** The coastline at Flamborough Head is one of the most spectacular areas of chalk cliff in Britain. Dramatic cliffs, some reaching 400ft (122m), thrust up out of the sea, providing a haven for wildlife. Thornwick Bay is just one of the many sheltered, shingle coves fronting the sea with caves and dramatic stacks. The old Beacon lighthouse at Flamborough was first built in 1674.

▶ **Bempton** One of the best-known nature reserves for seabirds in the UK, Bempton Cliffs is at the southern end of Filey Bay and was bought by the RSPB in 1969. Throughout the year more than a quarter of a million birds nest here. Puffin, guillemot and kittiwake abound on the cliffs and a major attraction is the huge gannet colony – the only nesting site for these birds on the British mainland. The best time to see the seabirds is during the nesting season in the summer, although visitors can enjoy bracing walks along the cliffs and visit the RSPB visitor centre throughout the year.

◀ **Humber Bridge** Opened in 1981, this beautiful suspension bridge was built to link north Lincolnshire and Humberside across the wide Humber estuary. Almost 1.5 miles long, the bridge has cut 50 miles off the road journey between the major ports of Hull and Grimsby. The south tower of the bridge is founded in shallow water 1,650ft (500m) from the shore.

▶ **The Deep** The striking glass and aluminium marine life centre called The Deep was conceived to educate visitors about the worlds' oceans. It stands at the confluence of the rivers Hull and Humber.

▲ **Spurn Head** Situated on the north bank of the entrance to the river Humber, this three-mile long finger of land that snakes out into the Humber estuary is constantly being reshaped by storms and coastal erosion. The distinctive black-and-white lighthouse became redundant in 1985 and has now been replaced by automatic beacons.

South Yorkshire

South Yorkshire ranges from high, bleak moorlands fringing the Peak District, through the densely populated area containing the city of Sheffield and the towns of Barnsley and Rotherham, to the fertile agricultural countryside beyond Doncaster to the east. The region contains many architectural and landscape gems including fine medieval, 18th century and Victorian buildings, public parks and country houses with their surrounding parks and gardens. In the west there are large sweeps of open country and elsewhere tracts of attractive walled, hedged and wooded farmed countryside.

◀ **Bradfield Moors** To the west of Sheffield are tracts of high moorland and upland pastures rising to more than 1,800ft (550m). No moorland can be bleaker or more beautiful, according to the season, than Bradfield Moors which stretch westwards from Bradfield village beyond Agden Reservoir.

▶ **Bradfield Church** There are two Bradfield villages, Low Bradfield and High Bradfield. Dominating High Bradfield is St Nicholas' parish church, one of the largest churches in Hallamshire. The churchyard contains some very old gravestones but most interesting is one dating from 1864 when the nearby Dale Dyke Reservoir burst its banks and the rushing torrent of water, pouring down the Loxley valley towards Sheffield, resulted in the death of 240 people.

▲ **Sheffield** The city centre is dominated by the Town Hall, built of Derbyshire sandstone, standing at the junction of Surrey Street and Pinstone Street. It was opened by Queen Victoria in 1897, who was greeted by Sheffield's first lord mayor, the Duke of Norfolk. Two friezes adorn the exterior walls; they depict grinders, smiths, smelters and miners. The 200ft tower has a bronze statue of Vulcan, the Roman god of fire and furnaces, with his right foot on an anvil and pincers in his left hand. On a sunny day, the Peace Gardens in front of the Town Hall provide a welcome green space for students and office-workers. The low curved roof on the far right is that of the Winter Gardens.

▲ **Barnsley Town Hall** Erected when Barnsley was the coal capital of South Yorkshire in 1932-33, it replaced the dingy old Town Hall in St Mary's Gate. Its imposing frontage, constructed from white limestone blocks, 21 bays long, is surmounted by an imposing clock tower. But it may not have ever had a clock tower – it was omitted from the final design on financial grounds and consent by the town council for its construction was only given at the last minute, four months after the foundation stone was laid. The cost of building and furnishing came to £188,000, an enormous figure in the depression days of the 1930s.

▼ **Roche Abbey** was founded in 1147 on a site given by two patrons, Richard de Busli and Richard Fitzurgis. It is a typical Cistercian site, tucked away in a secluded spot with a good water supply. Although only an inner gatehouse and the church transepts reach to any height, a complete Cistercian abbey plan is exposed in the ruins. In the 1770s Capability Brown was employed by the owner, the Earl of Scarbrough, to landscape the site and he covered up and planted over the ruins of the abbey. These have now been fully exposed to reveal the full abbey site.

◀ **Cusworth Hall** Owned by Doncaster Council, Cusworth Hall and Park were beautifully restored between 2004-7, partly funded by a £4.9m Heritage Lottery grant. William Wrightson (1676-1760) was the owner responsible for the building of the hall that stands today. The Rotherham mason-architect, George Platt, began to supervise the building of the new hall and on his death in 1742 his son, John, took over. Later extensions were designed by James Paine, the Palladian-style architect. William Wrightson's son-in-law, John Battie-Wrightson, commissioned Richard Woods, the landscape gardener, to improve the 100 acres of grounds surrounding the new hall between 1750-53. Features of the landscaped park dating from this period include three lakes, a bridge, a grotto-like boathouse and a cascade.